I0476016

The Art Of Packaging A Negotiation

How To Develop The Skill Of Assembling Potential Trades In Order To Get The Best Possible Outcome

"Practical, proven techniques that will help you get the best deal possible out of your next negotiation"

Dr. Jim Anderson

Published by:
Blue Elephant Consulting
Tampa, Florida

Copyright © 2017 by Dr. Jim Anderson

All rights reserved. No part of this book may be reproduced of transmitted in any form or by any means, electronic or mechanical, including photocopying, recording or by any information storage and retrieval system without written permission of the publisher, except for inclusion of brief quotations in a review.

Printed in the United States of America

Library of Congress Control Number: 2017901982

ISBN-13: 978-1542981392

ISBN-10: 1542981395

Warning – Disclaimer

The purpose of this book is to educate and entertain. This book does not promise or guarantee that anyone following the ideas, tips, suggestions, techniques or strategies will be successful. The author, publisher and distributor(s) shall have neither liability nor responsibility to anyone with respect to any loss or damage caused, or alleged to be caused, directly or indirectly by the information contained in this book.

Recent Books By The Author

Product Management

- Managing Your Product Manager Career: How Product Managers Can Find And Succeed In The Right Job

- How Product Managers Can Sell More Of Their Product: Tips & Techniques For Product Managers To Better Understand How To Sell Their Product

Public Speaking

- Creating Speeches That Work: How To Create A Speech That Will Make Your Message Be Remembered Forever!

- How To Organize A Speech In Order To Make Your Point: How to put together a speech that will capture and hold your audience's attention

CIO Skills

- How CIOs Can Bring Business And IT Together: How CIOs Can Use Their Technical Skills To Help Their Company Solve Real-World Business Problems

- New IT Technology Issues Facing CIOs: How CIOs Can Stay On Top Of The Changes In The Technology That

Powers The Company

IT Manager Skills

- How IT Managers Can Use New Technology To Meet Today's IT Challenges: Technologies That IT Managers Can Use In Order to Make Their Teams More Productive

- How To Build High Performance IT Teams: Tips And Techniques That IT Managers Can Use In Order To Develop Productive Teams

Negotiating

- Getting What You Want In A Negotiation By Learning How To Signal: How To Develop The Skill Of Effective Signaling In A Negotiation In Order To Get The Best Possible Outcome

- Exploring How To Get The Deal That You Want In A Negotiation: How To Develop The Skill Of Exploring What Is Possible In A Negotiation In Order To Reach The Best Possible Deal

Miscellaneous

- How To Heal A Broken Leg – Fast!: Understanding how to deal with a broken leg in order to start walking again quickly

- How Software Defined Networking (SDN) Is Going To Change Your World Forever: The Revolution In Network Design And How It Affects

Note: See a complete list of books by Dr. Jim Anderson at the back of this book.

Acknowledgements

Any book like this one is the result of years of real-world work experience. In my over 25 years of working for 7 different firms, I have met countless fantastic people and I've been mentored by some truly exceptional ones. Although I've probably forgotten some of the people who made me the person that I am today, here is my attempt to finally give them the recognition that they so truly deserve:

- Thomas P. Anderson
- Art Puett
- Bobbi Marshall
- Bob Boggs

Dr. Jim Anderson

This book is dedicated to my family: Lori, Maddie, Nick, and Ben. None of this would have been possible without their constant love and support.

Thanks for always believing in me and providing me with the strength to always be willing to go out there and be my best for you.

Speaking.   Negotiating.   Managing.   Marketing.

Table Of Contents

Package Your Negotiation To Get The Deal That You Want

During a negotiation a lot of promises and agreements are made by both sides of the table. This is all well and good, but the ultimate goal of any negotiation is for both sides to agree on a deal that they can live with. As a negotiator, it's going to be your job to take a look at where things stand in the negotiation and then package up the agreements so that they can be included in the final deal.

 As part of this process, you'll have to understand how delays can be used in a negotiation to get what you want. International negotiations can take a long time and be very complex, but they can show us how a deal can be packaged in a way that makes it agreeable to all.

Issues are what a negotiation is all about. As we look for ways to package a deal, we need to understand that there can be multiple solutions to each issue. Additionally, what we do for the other side or what they do for us can help to move things along.

Everything in a negotiation can have an effect on the bottom line of the deal that you are trying to package. You need to stay aware of this. In order to find the deal that both sides can live with, it helps to be able to focus on the long term.

Often times during a negotiation there can be so many things going on that it is all too easy to get lost and confused. That's why skilled negotiators use a checklist and a deal book. This allows them to keep track of all of the details and maintain a scoreboard that shows them who has agreed to what.

For more information on what it takes to be a great negotiator, check out my blog, The Accidental Negotiator, at:

www.TheAccidentalNegotiator.com

Good luck!

- Dr. Jim Anderson

About The Author

I must confess that I never set out to be a negotiator. When I went to school, I studied Computer Science and thought that I'd get a nice job programming and that would be that. Well, at least part of that plan worked out!

My first job was working for Boeing on their F/A-18 fighter jet program. I spent my days programming fighter jet software in assembly language and I loved it. The U.S. government decided to save some money and went looking for other countries to sell this plane to. This put me into an unfamiliar role: I started to negotiate with foreign military officials and I ended up having to participate in the negotiations for large international deals.

Time moved on and so did I. I found myself working for Siemens, the big German telecommunications company. They were making phone switches and selling them to the seven U.S. phone companies. The problem was that the switches were too complicated. When it came time to negotiate a deal with the customer, the sales teams struggled to create an effective negotiating strategy. I was called in to bridge the world between the product functionality and the business impacts as they related to the negotiations.

I've spent over 25 years working as a negotiator for both big companies and startups. This has given me an opportunity to learn what it takes to both plan and execute negotiations of all sizes. When it comes to negotiations, I've pretty much been there, done that.

I now live in Tampa Florida where I spend my time managing my consulting business, Blue Elephant Consulting, teaching college courses at the University of South Florida, and traveling to work with companies like yours to share the knowledge that I have about how to prepare for and execute successful negotiations.

I'm always available to answer questions and I can be reached at:

Dr. Jim Anderson
Blue Elephant Consulting
Email: jim@BlueElephantConsulting.com
Facebook: http://goo.gl/1TVoK
Web: **www.BlueElephantConsulting.com**

"Unforgettable communication skills that will set your ideas free…"

Create An Effective Negotiating Team At Your Company!

Dr. Jim Anderson is available to provide training and coaching on the topics that are the most important to people who have to negotiate: how can my team effectively prepare for and execute a successful negotiation that will get us what we both want and need?

Dr. Anderson believes that in order to both learn and remember what he says, audiences need to laugh. Each one of his speeches is full of fun and humor so that what he says "sticks" with everyone.

Dr. Anderson's Negotiating Training Includes:

1. How to plan for a negotiation: what information do you need and where can you find it?

2. What's the best way to explore how a deal can be created during a negotiation?

3. How can you bring a negotiation to a close without giving in to the other side?

Dr. Jim Anderson works with over 100 customers per year. To invite Dr. Anderson to work with you, contact him at:

Phone: 813-418-6970 or
Email: jim@BlueElephantConsulting.com

Blue
Elephant
Consulting
Speaking. Negotiating. Managing. Marketi

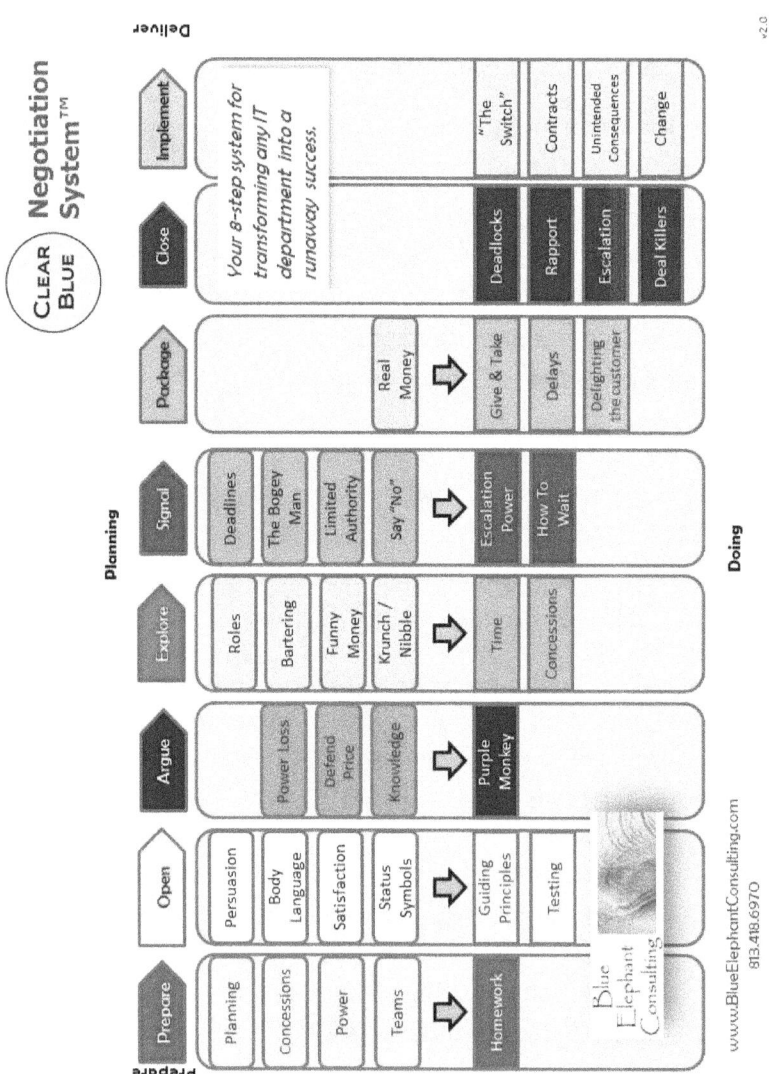

The **Clear Blue Negotiation System™** has been created to provide negotiators with a clear roadmap for how to manage a successful negotiation. This system shows negotiators what needs to be done and in what order to do it.

14

Chapter 1

The 2 Secret Ingredients To A Successful Negotiation

Chapter 1: The 2 Secret Ingredients To A Successful Negotiation

Whenever we go into the kitchen and decide to make a meal for ourselves, the first thing that we do is to get all of the ingredients that we're going to need out and assembled so that we'll be able to find them when we need them. It turns out that the strategy for conducting a successful negotiation is very similar to this. **We need to have the correct ingredients if we want to be able to create a deal that both sides will be able to live with**. Two of the most critical ingredients are enthusiasm and relationships.

The Power Of Genuine Enthusiasm

Let's face it – if you are entering into a negotiation, then **you are really playing the role of a salesperson**. This means that no matter what negotiation styles or negotiating techniques are being used, you are going to have to get the other side of the table excited about what you have to sell to them. In order for this to happen, you're going to have to bring your enthusiasm to the table.

The great thing about enthusiasm is that **it is contagious**. Just by being enthusiastic you'll be able to cause the other side to also become enthusiastic about the deal that is being negotiated. What makes this technique even more amazing is that it works on everyone – even those people who consider themselves to be your adversaries.

Ultimately, your enthusiasm has to come from your belief in your own ideas. During any negotiation a great number of objections will probably be raised. It's going to be up to your enthusiasm and your ability to **sell your ideas to the other side** in order to overcome everything that stands in the way of your reaching a deal with the other side.

Building Relationships Is What Makes A Deal Work

What is **the most important part of any negotiation?** A lot of people will tell you that it's all about the money. They look at the profit that they'll make from doing a deal and it's their belief that if they can just negotiate the right price, then everything else associated with the deal will line up. It turns out that this is not the case.

Instead, what is really important is the type of personal relationship that you'll be able to build with the other side of the table during the negotiations. This is going to be a critical factor in helping you to reach a successful conclusion in the current negotiation. Additionally, you will probably have future negotiations with these people and **the relationship that you build today will help you tomorrow**.

All too often beginning negotiators believe that they need to make promises to the other side in order to get them to agree to things. This isn't correct. Instead, **take the time to find common ground between you and the other side** and then use this to convince them that they can trust you. By doing this, you won't have to sell the other side on your ideas, instead they'll believe what you tell them because they believe in you.

What All Of This Means For You

Every principled negotiation that you participate in is a creation that you've made. Just like creating a delicious meal, **you've got to bring the right ingredients** to the negotiating table if you want to create a deal that works for both sides. Two of the ingredients that every negotiation must have are enthusiasm and relationships.

Your enthusiasm is contagious. If the other side sees how committed you are to reaching a deal with them, they'll become motivated to find a way to make the deal work. Likewise, you need to move beyond price and take the time to create a relationship with the other side of the table. You never know when you'll be back at the negotiating table working on another deal with them.

Both of these ingredients, enthusiasm and relationships, are critical components of any negotiation that is going to produce a deal that both sides can live with. Take the time to enter a negotiation with a lot of genuine enthusiasm and work to build a solid relationship with the other side. Doing this **will help you to reach the deal that you both want more quickly**.

Chapter 2

The Power Of Delays In A Negotiation

Chapter 2: The Power Of Delays In A Negotiation

We all hate delays, right? No matter if it is when we are in traffic, waiting in a line at a store, or waiting for the next web page to load, **any sort of delay is a bad thing**. Or is it? It turns out that in a negotiation, sometimes a delay can be a very good thing. We just have to learn how best to deal with them.

How To Use A Delay In A Negotiation

Every negotiation has its own timeline. Every negotiation follows a somewhat standard path of starting, wandering around for a while, and then moving towards either a successful conclusion or aborts. As is the case with the rest of life, **delays can enter into any negotiation** at any time. This is where an opportunity may make itself available to you.

You have the ability to slow down the negotiation at any point in time. When you do this, **the other side will react**. Their reaction will tell you a great deal about their situation. They may start to complain that the negotiation is now taking too long. If they do, then you now have an opportunity to renegotiate what they would like to trade speed for: more money, a better delivery schedule, etc.

What this means for you is that if the other side of the table tells you that they can't handle any delay in the negotiations, then **you now have more negotiating power**. Their only choice at this point in time, outside of walking away, is to make concessions to you in order to get the negotiations back on track.

How To Build A Fire Under The Other Side In A Negotiation

However, in a negotiation, you may not be the only one who is slowing things down – the other side of the table may have decided to delay the negotiations. If this happens, then you are going to have to **find a way to motivate them to speed things up**.

The **type of motivation that you choose to use** will depend on the negotiation that you are currently involved in. It could be you reducing the price of your product, it could be a change in some aspect of the timing associated with the deal, or it could mean you walking away from the deal altogether.

Ultimately you are going to have to develop **your own personal sense of timing** for each negotiation that you are involved in. You are going to have to be able to detect when a delay is occurring and you'll need to be able to evaluate your options on what steps you would like to take in order to get things moving once again.

What All Of This Means For You

In any principled negotiation there are a wide variety of negotiation styles and negotiating techniques that can be used. In addition, **delays are another tool** that an experienced negotiator can use to control the flow of the negotiation.

Every negotiation has a timeline associated with it. You can control how the other side of the table behaves by either **delaying the negotiation** or working around a delay that they are causing. When the timeline starts to deviate from what the other side wants, they will become more willing to make concessions in order to get it back on track.

The ability to understand how best to use delays is something that comes with negotiating experience. Once you have this you'll know how to get your next negotiation to **move towards your ultimate goal at the correct speed**.

Chapter 3

Negotiating With Iran: How Was A Deal Reached?

Chapter 3: Negotiating With Iran: How Was A Deal Reached?

It is through negotiation that **the impossible can be made possible** no matter what negotiation styles or negotiating techniques are being used. A deal has been brokered between Iran and the rest of the world in regards to their work on creating an atomic bomb. For more than a decade Iran has been willing to put up with crippling international sanctions in order to continue to pursue its goal of creating an atomic weapon. However, recently everything has changed. How were the negotiators able to create a deal?

Change Opens New Doors In Negotiation

The reports on the state of Iran's nuclear program have always been mixed. Research has been going on since 2003. A 2011 report by the International Atomic Energy Agency (IAEA) Board of Governors seem to indicate that Iran had started to perform specific tests that were designed to allow it to **start to create nuclear weapons**.

For years Iran has been engaged in a significant government backed program to develop nuclear weapons. They had made no secret of their plans. The world had reacted to this by **levying significant sanctions against Iran**. Life in Iran had become very difficult for many of its citizens; however, the Iranian president Mahmoud Ahmadinejad, was deeply committed to the country's nuclear program for a variety of reasons.

The election in June of 2013 in Iran has ushered in Hassan Rouhani as the country's new president. As with all change, **this opened the door to a new round of negotiations**. The West saw this change in government leadership as a new opportunity to

24

try to determine if there was a possibility to negotiate an end to Iran's nuclear ambitions.

Using A Two-Track Negotiation Strategy

These types of negotiations are always tricky to do – the spotlight of world attention would be on them. Within all of the countries involved in the negotiations, Iran especially, there would be **many powerful forces** who would be both for and against any deal being reached.

The U.S. played a key role in having the sanctions imposed on Iran and they would have to play a major role in any deal that would be reached. The U.S. had decided to **peruse a two-track negotiating strategy**. One track would be the one that was done publically – every step of the process would be reported in the papers and discussed endlessly on television. The other would be done in secret.

At the direction of the U.S. president, Barack Obama, the U.S. had been secretly reaching out Iran for the past 5 years. In August of 2013 things started to move faster after a letter was delivered from President Obama to Iran's new president Hassan Rouhani. The secret talks were designed to build a foundation that would allow the public talks to move forward. The secret negotiations were successful in **creating the elements of a deal** and resolving the differences between Iran and the world powers. With the recent announcements that a deal has been struck, it's clear that this two-track negotiating strategy has paid off.

What All Of This Means For You

The leadership of the country of Iran has finally agreed to a deal in which they will **halt their development of nuclear weapons** in exchange for having international sanctions against them lifted. This is an amazing event because for the past decade no such agreement had been possible.

The reason that negotiators were able to reach this deal now was because of **changes that have occurred within Iran** and the negotiating strategy that was used. Iran has a new president who has come into power promising that he would make changes that would make life easier for the citizens of Iran. Getting the international sanctions lifted is a key part of this. The negotiating teams knew that they needed to create a foundation for the negotiations to use. A secret two-track negotiating scheme was used to allow this foundation to be created.

Every principled negotiation can be judged by the results that it creates. The negotiations between Iran and the rest of the world have been nothing if not miraculous. What had seemed to be out of reach for so long is now almost a reality. The ability of the negotiators to continue to negotiate for such a long time clearly goes to show that in negotiating, **it's not over until it's over!**

Chapter 4

The Power Of Favors During A Negotiation

Chapter 4: The Power Of Favors During A Negotiation

In a negotiation we want the other side of the table to make concessions to us so that we can get what we need out of the negotiations. However, in all honesty, no matter what negotiation styles or negotiating techniques we use, they probably are really not all that motivated to **give us the concessions that we want**. What this means for us is that we're going to have to find a way to get them to want to give us what we both want and need. Hmm, how can we make this happen?

One Good Turn Deserves Another

When we want the other side of the table to make a concession to us, there are a lot of different ways to go about making this happen. One that comes to mind right away is to **force them to give in to us**. In some cases we might be able to do this; however, the rest of the negotiation just got a lot harder because now they are going to be resenting us.

A much better way to get what we want out of a negotiation is to **make the other side want to make a concession to us**. One of the best ways to go about making this happen is to use the "one good turn deserves another" technique. Note that this is very different from the concept of a "freebie" – in this case you are not giving something away. Rather, you are doing something for the other side and you expect them to then do something for you.

The key to making this technique work for you is that **you need to know what issues that are being negotiated are important to you** and which ones are not. You are going to want to give in to the other side on a number of the unimportant issues and then ask them to give in to you on one of the important issues.

How To Be A Good Negotiator

You'll never be able to get your way on every issue in a negotiation. A good negotiator knows that he or she is going to have to **exchange some minor losses for some major wins**.

Using this technique where you give in on minor issues to get them to give in on major issues is how you get the other side **to be willing to make the concessions that you want them to make**. What a good negotiator realizes is that not all issues are equal – the exchange of concessions does not have to include items of equal value.

An example of this would be if you gave in on five different items and then **asked the other side to give in on one**. Those five items may have had very little value to you, but the one that you want them to give in to you on might be a very big deal to you. Make sure that you keep the value that you place on the different items that are being negotiated hidden from the other side.

What All Of This Means For You

Getting the other side of the table to give us what we want is what negotiations are all about. It's how to make this happen that is **the hard thing to do**.

The key to getting the concessions from the other side that you want is to **make concessions to them**. Give in on the little issues that you really don't care about, let these mount up and then ask them to give in on something that you really do care about. Don't be afraid to make concessions to the other side. This is all part of the process and you'll need to give in order to get.

Skilled negotiators realize that **a principled negotiation is all about both giving and getting**. Taking the time to give into the other side will allow you to get them to give in to you on the issues that, in the end, really matter to you. Learn how to do this and you'll be the negotiator who always gets what you want from a negotiation.

Chapter 5

Every Negotiating Issue Has Multiple Solutions

Chapter 5: Every Negotiating Issue Has Multiple Solutions

Although I'm sure that many of us have heard about negotiations that got hopelessly deadlocked, it turns out that in most cases a negotiation can always be kept on track so that you can reach a deal with the other side no matter what negotiation styles or negotiating techniques are being used. **The key is to understand that you always have the power** – you could walk away from the deal if you had to. Since we never want to do that, what we need to do is to understand how to work flexibility into our next negotiation so that we can find the multiple solutions that will work for us.

Keeping The Other Side At The Table

In order to conduct a successful negotiation, you are going to need to have both parties come to the table and stay at the table. That may sound easy, but during a heated negotiation, one or both parties may decide that it's time to throw in the towel. As a negotiator, **you need to take steps in order to make sure that this doesn't happen**.

Look, if during a negotiation you reach the conclusion that the situation is hopeless – you are never going be able to reach a deal with the other side, then yes, you need to give up and walk away. However, before you do this you need to realize that both disagreements with the other side and actual deadlocks **are really opportunities for you to create a different type of deal**. You need to remain flexible and keep an open mind when you encounter these situations.

It is entirely possible that during a negotiation things will start to go off the track when the other side starts to become angry. You can tell that this is happening when they start to interrupt you, raise their voice, or start to lose patience with what is going on. If this happens, then **you need to start to communicate to the other side that you are flexible**; you are willing to search for different ways to resolve the issues. As long as you can keep the discussions going, then both sides will be in a position to remain flexible.

Different Aspects Of Flexibility

I'm often asked by novice negotiators what flexibility actually looks like in a negotiation. The answer, of course, is that it depends. There is not one thing that you can point at and say "that's evidence of flexibility", rather it has a tendency to **sneak into a negotiation from around the corners**.

Flexibility can enter into a negotiation in several different ways. The first is in how you choose to define the bottom line. **The definition that you use when the negotiations start may not be the definition that you'll be using when things wrap up**. Additionally, we need to understand that in any negotiation there is both an apparent and a real bottom line. What both sides may see as being the bottom line may only be the apparent bottom line at the start of the negotiations. Based on the discussions that you have, the real bottom line will emerge.

Different kinds of flexibility may be used during a negotiation. What many of us don't realize is that a negotiation is really an opportunity for us to **use our trial and error skills**. If we are trying something and it's not working out for us, then that is a message that we need to go back and try something else. Your goal has to be to keep trying different things until you achieve the deal that you've been looking for.

What All Of This Means For You

The wrong way to approach your next principled negotiation is to go in thinking that there is **one and only one solution that is**

going to provide you with the deal that you want. What you need to do is to negotiate with flexibility so that you are able adjust your approach and stay on track.

The first thing that you'll need to do is to **remain flexible** when the other side of the table starts to become upset. You'll need to find ways to keep them talking and get them to calm down. Keep in mind that there are a number of different aspects to negotiating flexibility and each can be used when appropriate.

The most important thing to keep in mind when you enter into your next negotiation is that there are **many different ways to reach a deal that will meet your needs**. You need to retain the flexibility that will allow you to adjust your position and work with the other side to take new paths that will lead you to a deal.

Chapter 6

When You Are Negotiating, It's All About The Bottom Line

Chapter 6: When You Are Negotiating, It's All About The Bottom Line

So how is that negotiation going? Generally, speaking, no matter what negotiation styles or negotiating techniques are being used, we judge our negotiating success with **how the bottom line is looking**. The bottom line is more often than not evaluated in financial terms. This is how most of us have been trained to evaluate a bottom line and therefore a negotiation. However, it turns out that we might be doing this all wrong. There are other things that we need to be considering...

A Financial Bottom Line Has Many Different Aspects

Ok, so hopefully we are all on board when it comes to understanding just exactly what a financial bottom line is – the price that one side of the negotiation is going to agree to pay. It turns out that if you look at it correctly, **the financial bottom line actually includes much more than this**.

Sure the price is included in the bottom line. However, what is also included but what is not always considered as much is the financing that will be used, the payment terms that have been agreed to, and any extra conditions that have been included. Reaching an agreement with the other side of the table can be difficult not because of the bottom line price, but rather **because of all of these other factors**.

From a negotiator point of view, when we are thinking about the financial bottom line it is possible that we're thinking about the wrong thing. Sure, **the price does matter**. However, what might be even more important than how much something costs is what does this deal include?

How To Use Marketing To Make Your Bottom Line Even Better

When you are involved in a negotiation where the other side has its attention fixed on the price, **you may find yourself with a unique opportunity**. In this type of negotiating situation, you may be able to negotiate a number of concessions that you would not normally be able to get in exchange for being flexible on the price.

You need to keep in mind that **any deal consists of a lot more than just the price**. Marketing and all of the things that are associated with it are things that lend themselves to being included in any negotiation. What you are able to get the other side to agree to in terms of marketing issues may end up having a greater impact on the deal than the price did.

When you are negotiating, you always need to be keeping your eyes open for **new opportunities** to make the deal even better for you. Keep in mind the fact that you may need to convince the other side that doing business with you is their only option. Get them to agree to this concept, and they will become less focused on the financial bottom line and more focused on reaching a good deal with you.

What All Of This Means For You

Negotiators always want to know how a principled negotiation is going. One method that we use to accomplish this is by **taking a look at the bottom line in financial terms**. However, it turns out that by doing this we may be short-sighted. It turns out that there are a number of different aspects to the bottom line that we need to account for.

The bottom line is important in any deal; however, what may be even more important is **what the deal includes or does not**

include. Part of this might be how and when the money will exchange hands. If the other side of the table is focused on the price, you may be able to use this to your advantage. You may be able to get a number of additional concessions as a result of your willingness to be flexible on the price.

Yes, the financial bottom line of any negotiation is important. However, it turns out that if you focus too much on just that part of a negotiation then you'll quickly run into problems. Keep in mind that a bottom line **has many different aspects** and that you may really want marketing concessions instead of a lower price. Watch your bottom line and you'll be able to get the best deal possible.

Chapter 7

Learn To Think Long-Term In Your Next Negotiation

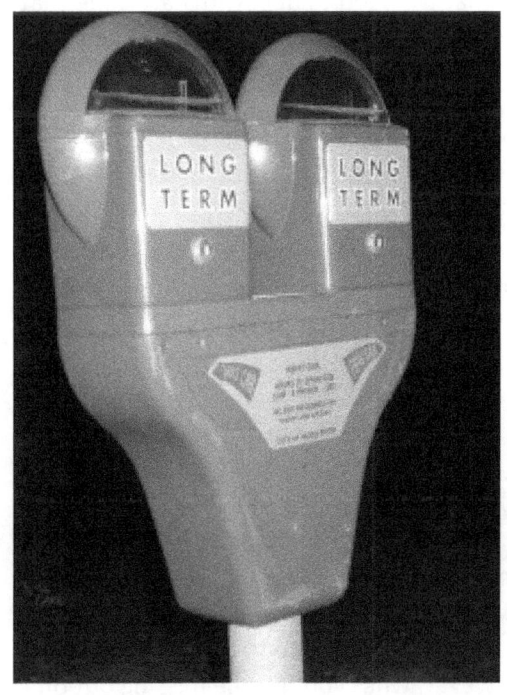

Chapter 7: Learn To Think Long-Term In Your Next Negotiation

When we enter into a negotiation, it can be very easy for us to focus our attention on the deal that is on the table before us. After all, this is why we are spending the time on this negotiation and getting the deal that we want is why we have spent our time collecting information while we prepared. However, it turns out that if we can shift our thinking from the short-term to long-term **we may end up walking away from the negotiations with a much better deal.**

The Power Of Thinking Long-Term

All of this short-term / long-term talk brings us to the fundamental question that we need to deal with each time that we start a negotiation: **what do you really want to get out of this negotiation?** That's a good question and all too often I believe that we may not have a complete answer to this question.

Yes, there will always be some fundamental issues that are on the table in front of us. In fact, the negotiation that we are now involved in was probably advertised as being all about these very issues. However, if we believe that these issues are what this negotiation is all about then our thinking is very much **short-term thinking.**

The problem with entering into a negotiation with only short-term thinking is that you are going to spend the entire negotiation **focused on just the issues that are on the table**. The negotiation styles and negotiating techniques that you'll use will all be based on trying to get the best deal relative to those issues. If this is all that there was to this negotiation, then that would be fine. However, what you may be missing out on is the power of thinking long-term.

How To Think Long-Term

The really good negotiators are always able to take a step back from the table and **think about what they want to accomplish in the long-term**. What this means is to realize that the issues that are on the table may be important, but they may not be as important as what you'd like to accomplish in the long term.

One example of this would be **if you were selling a house**. You might be negotiating with the other side over the price that you'd be willing to sell the house for. Now you know that if you had the money from the sale of the house today, you could use it to buy gold which you think will dramatically increase in value over the next week. Instead of trying to get the highest price for your house, you might be willing to settle for a lower price in order to quickly complete the deal and get paid because you know in the long-term you'll end up making more money.

It's this ability to keep your eye on the long term objectives that can **make you a better negotiator**. When you are able to be aware of what you really want to accomplish in the long-term, it makes you more flexible in the short term. You'll be willing to give in on issues in the negotiation that you might not have been willing to do so because you have the long-term view.

What All Of This Means For You

The most important thing about any principled negotiation that we are involved in is to make sure that **we know what we want to get out of the negotiation**. It can be easy for us to get distracted by the immediate short-term goals that are on the table. However, the real value of the negotiation may come from the long-term objectives that we can achieve.

When you are able to focus on the long-term benefits that you can get out of a negotiation, **you are able to become more**

flexible in the details of the negotiation. Because you are aware of what this negotiation can provide you with in terms of the big picture, you may become more willing to make concessions on short-term issues that won't matter as much in the long-term.

It's this ability to understand the big picture that can **transform your negotiating skills**. Instead of feeling the need to "win" every negotiation that you are in, you'll be able to understand that "winning" may actually mean appearing to get a worse deal in the short-term. However, in the long-term it will become clear that you were the better negotiator.

Chapter 8

Why Negotiators Should Put A Dead Dog On The Table

Chapter 8: Why Negotiators Should Put A Dead Dog On The Table

Our goal as negotiators in our next negotiation is to **get the other side of the table to agree to our proposals** no matter what negotiation styles or negotiating techniques are being used. Unfortunately, all too often they don't like what we are proposing and they decide to hold out to see if they can get us to offer them a better deal. We'd really like to find a way to prevent this from happening. Thats exactly where placing a dead dog on the negotiating table just might help you to get what you want...

Say Hello To Your Dead Dog

So here's the problem that all too often we come face-to-face with in a negotiation: **the other side wants more from us**. Specifically, the deal that has currently been offered to them is not enough – they believe that they can get more from us. The reasons for this thinking can be many, but generally this happens early on in a negotiation and our initial offer is always seen as that – an initial offer.

We can't allow this to happen. We need a strategy that will convince the other side **to accept our offer**. One way to make this happen is for you to bring a dead dog to the negotiation and place it on the negotiating table. No, no, no – I'm not talking about actually placing a dead dog on the table. Instead, what I'm going to suggest that you do is to present the other side with a deal that you just know that they'll never accept.

Once you do this, **fight very hard to get them to accept it**. Pull out all of the stops – tell them that this is the deal that you just must have. Cry, pound your fists, yell, do whatever you think is necessary to get them to say "yes". Of course, they won't.

When you finally reach a point where you've tried everything and they just have not budged, now is the time to give in.

It's Always Good To Have A Backup Plan

The reason that you made this proposal that you knew that they would never accept was because **you wanted to set the stage for the proposal that you do want them to accept**. The second proposal that you'll make to them is the one that you want them to accept; however, they won't know that. When you finally do present your second proposal to the other side, they'll be thrilled to see it simply because it will appear to be so much more reasonable than your first proposal.

This is what is called **the "dead dog on the table" strategy**. Getting the other side to accept the proposal that you really wanted them to accept is a well proven strategy. What's being used here is called the negotiating "theory of relativity" – the second proposal appears to be acceptable in relation to the first one. Because you made a concession to them by eventually being willing to walk away from your dead dog proposal, they'll feel even more obligated to accept your second proposal.

What All Of This Means For You

The one thing that we would really like to avoid in our next principled negotiation is **having the other side reject our proposal** because they think that we'll make them better offer. In order to prevent this from happening, sometimes it's a good move to place a dead dog on the negotiating table.

By this I mean that you should make an outrageous proposal to the other side that you know that they'll never accept. You then need to argue very passionately to see if you can get them to accept it – and they won't. Eventually, you'll give in and then **you'll make an alternative proposal** that they'll quickly accept because they see how reasonable it is in comparison to your dead dog proposal.

This careful manipulation of the other side is very legal. What you are really trying to do is to open their eyes to **just how reasonable the deal that you want them to agree to is**. By using the dead dog approach you can streamline the negotiating process and get to a final deal quicker than you would otherwise. Who would have ever thought that a dead dog could be so useful?

Chapter 9

Why Every Negotiator Should Have A "Deal Book"

Chapter 9: Why Every Negotiator Should Have A "Deal Book"

Let's face it: negotiating is a complicated process even before you start thinking about all of the negotiation styles and negotiating techniques that are involved. There may a number of different people involved, you may be discussing many different issues, and don't even get me started on all of the dates and places that can be involved. Needless to say, it can be very difficult for a single person to keep all of this straight before, during, and after a negotiation. **That's why we all need some help**. That's why we all need a "deal book".

What Is A Deal Book?

So, if this deal book thing is so important, perhaps we should take a closer look at exactly what it is. One way to view a deal book is to think of it as being sort of a general ledger where you **keep track of everything that has to do with a negotiation** that will be happening in the future. Instead of a host of post-it notes, files on your laptop, or scribbled sheets of paper, instead everything having to do with the upcoming negotiation is always in one and only one place.

I'm sure that you are proud of just how many details about a given negotiation you are able to store in your head. However, I'm also willing to bet that **you can't keep it all up there**. This is where the deal book comes in. You're going to have to use your deal book to keep track of such things as who you've called in setting up the negotiation, who called you about the negotiation, what was agreed to, etc.

As you can start to see, the deal book is going to be **a key tool** in helping you get ready for your next negotiation. In fact, if you are going to be negotiating as a part of a team, your deal book is going to be a critical tool for everyone. This means that as you make updates to your deal book, you are going to have to get those updates transcribed and passed on to the rest of your team so that everyone is in the loop.

How Do You Use A Deal Book?

Having a deal book is a good first step; however, it's **how you choose to use your deal book that will provide you with an advantage over the other side of the table**. Your deal book will help you to keep track of things as you prepare for the upcoming negotiation. You can use it to record on a day-by-day basis all of the people that you are talking with to schedule the negotiation, their telephone numbers, and any action items that you need to take care of before the negotiations start.

Many negotiators have **very specific rules** for what their deal books look like and how they are treated. The experienced ones tend to favor using a spiral bound notebook as opposed to a loose leaf notebook. Losing or misplacing your deal book would be a serious loss. In order to make sure that this never happens, most negotiators insist that it always occupy a specific place on their desk. This way when they need it, they never have to go looking for it.

Used correctly, your deal book will contain a complete list of **what you've told the other side and what their response to you was**. This can come in handy later in the negotiations. If during the negotiations they say something that contradicts what they've already told you, you'll be able to look it up in your deal book and resolve the discrepancy.

What All Of This Means For You

We negotiators are always looking for a way to get better. It turns out that using what is called a "deal book" is how the professional negotiators **keep everything straight** during those long and involved negotiations that have so many different details associated with them. We need to start using deal books.

A deal book can physically be just about anything. The pros like to use spiral notebooks so that they can't lose any pages. A deal book is used to **keep track of all of the details that are needed in order to prepare for a principled negotiation** . This includes calls made, calls received, telephone numbers, and who said what. All of this information can become critical during the negotiation if the other side says something that contradicts what they said before the negotiations started. You'll have your notes and so you can get things straightened out if this happens.

You wouldn't think that something as simple as a notebook could have such a big impact on how a negotiation turns out. However, it's not just a notebook – **it's a deal book**. Take the time to create your own deal book and use it as you prepare for your next negotiation. You just might be surprised at how much power it puts in your hands!

Chapter 10

Negotiators Need Both A Checklist And An Organizer

Chapter 10: Negotiators Need Both A Checklist And An Organizer

Every negotiator should be **using a deal book** in order to keep track of all of the 100's of tiny details that go on in every negotiation. So that you don't forget or overlook anything, your deal book can act as both a checklist for the negotiation and as an organizer for your thoughts. Deciding to do this is a great first step, the challenge comes when you sit down to do it – just exactly how do you use this thing?

What Goes Into A Deal Book To Help Organize A Negotiation?

So let's say that you've got yourself a deal book (really just a spiral bound notebook). Now what? Many of the negotiators that I talk with are baffled as to exactly **what they need to do with their deal book** in order to get the maximum benefit from it.

At its heart, a deal book is where you keep your records about your next negotiation. What this means for you is that as you start to prepare for the negotiation, **everything that happens gets its own place in your deal book**. This will include such things as you taking time to write down what you hope to get out of the negotiations, any and all telephone numbers and addresses of the people who will be involved in the negotiations, and every piece of random info about the negotiations that you happen to pick up.

The list of what you can record in your deal book is actually quite lengthy. It can include such items as the dates and places where negotiations occurred. You'd want to note down who participated in the negotiations on a given date. During the negotiation, there will of course be **open issues that are**

currently not resolved. Your deal book is a great place to note these so that you are aware of what has been resolved and what still needs to be taken care of.

How Do You Use A Deal Book As A Checklist?

Your deal book is where you get an opportunity to keep a running diary of how the negotiation is going. When new information is learned, **you should note it in your deal book**. Additionally, how you react to this new information should also be noted.

Your goals for the negotiation should be a part of your deal book. By doing this, you can create a checklist of what you want to get out of the negotiations. As you achieve your individual goals, you can start to check off each one of them. With a little luck by the end of the negotiation you'll have eventually completed your entire checklist.

One of the most important uses of your deal book checklist is **when there is a need for someone else to take over a negotiation**. There can be many reasons that this happens, but generally it can cause a great deal of confusion on both sides of the table and often sets the negotiations back a bit. However, if you can hand your deal book off to the person who is taking over, then they will be able to quickly come up to speed on where things stand and what has already been done. You improve their odds of being able to successfully reach the negotiation goals that you had set for yourself.

What Does All Of This Mean For You?

Each and every principled negotiation that we are involved in, no matter how large it may appear to be from the outside or what negotiation styles or negotiating techniques are being used, is a complex beast. With multiple people involved, different dates, agreements, and deliverables **things can get pretty complicated very quickly**. What every negotiator needs in order to keep things organized is a deal book.

A deal book allows all of the details having to do with a negotiation to be **kept in one place**. In the deal book you can keep track of dates, places, participants, and meeting agendas. Additionally, using a well-kept deal book allows the planning and execution of a negotiation to be traded off among different people without the loss of any information.

No, creating and maintaining a deal book is not easy to do. However, **the benefits are huge**. For the next negotiation that you will be involved in take the time to create a deal book that will help you organize your negotiation and which can be used as a checklist. When you're able to walk away with the deal that you wanted, you'll be able to thank your deal book.

Chapter 11

Chapter 11: In Negotiating, It's Really All About The Details...

Chapter 11: In Negotiating, It's Really All About The Details...

Let's face it, negotiating can be a very tricky thing to do well what with all of the different negotiation styles and negotiating techniques that are used. There are a lot of different reasons why negotiating can be hard to do, but one of the biggest is that **there are just so many different things that you have to keep track of**. The really good negotiators have found a way to do this, perhaps we should start doing what they do...?

Use A Deal Book To Keep Track Of The Details

The deal that you want to get out of your next negotiation will be the result of how you come to agreement on a number of different details. Not all of the details will be of the same size (there will be small details and large details) and they will not all be of the same importance (there will be more important ones and less important ones). However, **they will all be important to your ability to create a deal that both sides can live with**.

What this means for you is that you are going to have to **start to use a deal book** to keep track of everything that is going on in your negotiations. Ultimately what you are going to want to create is a checklist that you can use to keep track of the points that have been discussed during your negotiation.

What you are going to be trying to track will be what has already been agreed to and **what negotiation items you consider to still be open**. For the open items, you are going to want to maintain a separate list of what you think is going to be required in order to create a solution to these open items. Ultimately, by creating this checklist you are going to be able to both track and organize the status of your negotiation as it moves from start to finish.

Every Claim Has To Be Checked Out

During a negotiation, both sides are going to be making claims in order to generate support for their position in the negotiation. That's all fine and good; however, every time the other side makes a claim you are going to have the responsibility of **checking it out** to ensure that it's valid.

During a typical negotiation there will ultimately be a fair number of these claims that you are going to end up having to check out. Once again, your negotiation deal book is going to come in handy here. When a claim is made, you are going to have to **take the time to properly document the claim**.

Just writing a claim down is not enough. You are going to have to **create a "to-do" list** related to all of the claims that the other side has made. As you take the time to check out each of the claims that has been made, you can start to check off each item on your check off list. It is also possible that as the negotiations proceed, some of the items on this list may become either unimportant or no longer required.

What All Of This Means For You

When you sit down to negotiate with the other side of the table, you are **accepting responsibility** for both managing a lot of details and checking out a lot of claims. This may sound like a lot of work, it is. However, if you want to be a successful negotiator, then you are going to have to master both of these tasks.

The good news is that you are probably already using the tool that you'll need in order to take care of both of these items. The deal book that most negotiators use to keep track of everything that is going on in a principled negotiation **will help you to stay on top of all of the negotiation details**. Additionally, when the

57

other side makes a claim, your deal book will allow you to create a checklist that you can use to check out and verify all of their claims.

No, the use of a deal book is not going to make your next negotiation any easier. However, it is going to **boost your chances of not overlooking any details** or not checking out any claims. Just this alone should help you to feel that you have a better grasp of what's going on in the negotiations. Use these suggestions to make sure that you are able to reach the best deal possible in your next negotiation!

Chapter 12

Every Negotiation Needs A Scorecard

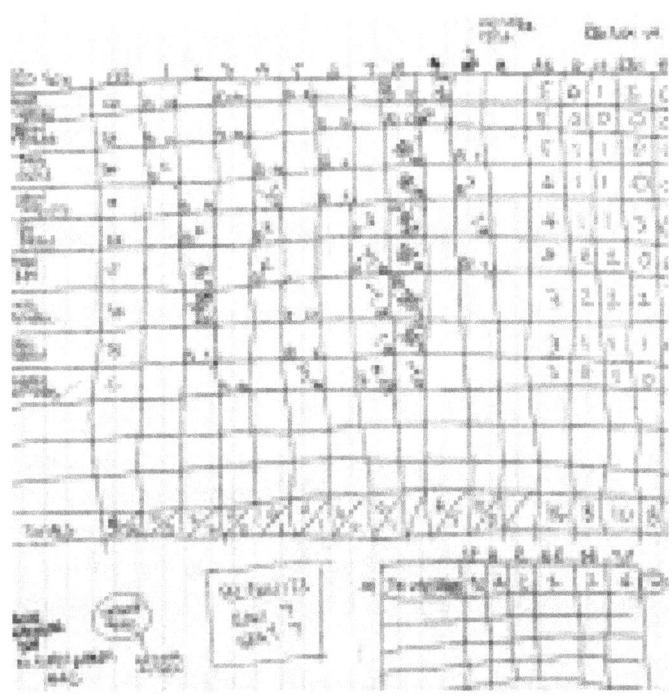

Chapter 12: Every Negotiation Needs A Scorecard

I can only speak for myself, but when I'm involved in a detailed negotiation, things can get pretty confusing very quickly with all of the different negotiation styles and negotiating techniques that are being used. There are a lot of different issues that need to be resolved as a part of reaching an agreement with the other side of the table and the more people who are participating in the negotiation, the more complicated things can get. The best way that I've discovered for dealing with complex negotiations and not getting lost is for me to use a negotiation scorecard.

What Is A Negotiation Scorecard?

I'm pretty sure that even if you are not a big sports fan, you probably still know what a scorecard is – it's how you can tell who is ahead in a game. In a negotiation in which there are many different issues that will all need to be resolved, a scorecard is simply a system that you can use to understand where things currently stand. By using a scorecard you should be able to tell how close you are to reaching the conclusion of the negotiations.

A negotiation scorecard does not have to be a complex thing. I like to use Microsoft Excel to build a simple side-by-side listing of each of the points that we are going to be discussing during an upcoming negotiation. I then go back and I document the differences in the positions of the two parties that are involved in the negotiations.

The power of using a scorecard comes from the fact that once you have created it, you will then be able to see at a glance all of the different areas that are going to require resolution in order for both sides to be able to reach an agreement. With this list, you can then prioritize what issues you want to work on (this is why I keep track of my list in Excel!). The easy ones should be very obvious and the ones that are going to require more work and perhaps some compromises will also stand out.

How Do You Use A Negotiation Scorecard?

In order for a negotiation scorecard to be useful to you during a negotiation, it is going to have to be comprehensive. If you can include everything that will be discussed on your scorecard, then you'll discover that even the biggest and most scary negotiations can be transformed into a manageable and finite list of things to be accomplished.

Once you've created you scorecard, you may want to share it with the other side of the table. If you do, you'll want to ask them "Does my scorecard contain everything that we want to discuss? If we were able to resolve all of these issues, would we be able to reach a deal?" By getting them to agree to this, you will have bounded your negotiation and will have assured yourself that you fully understand what needs to be accomplished.

One of the things that can cause a negotiation to go on and on is when there is "issue creep". The other side keeps adding things to the negotiations that were never there in the first place. By creating a scorecard and getting the other side to agree that its contents are complete you can prevent issue creep from happening. If the other side attempts to add another issue to the negotiations, you can get your scorecard out and ask them "...but you agreed that these were all of the issues that we needed to resolve, where did this new issue come from?"

What Does All Of This Mean For You?

Negotiations can be complicated beasts. As mere humans, we can often struggle to try and keep everything straight – what has already been agreed to and what issues do we still need to resolve? The good news is that there are tools available to us that can help us get this situation under control. If we create a negotiation scorecard, we can keep track of where the negotiation is currently at.

A scorecard is nothing more than a side-by-side list of the issues that will be discussed during the negotiations. Seeing everything that will need to be resolved in order to reach a deal can help you to understand where you'll need to spend your time. Getting the other side to agree that your scorecard is complete can help to prevent issue creep from happening and delaying the conclusion of your negotiation.

As negotiators we are always looking for ways that we can boost our odds of getting the best deal possible out of our next principled negotiation. Scorecards are one way that even when we are involved in complex negotiations we can keep track of where things are at and what it's going to take to wrap things up. Try using a scorecard with your next negotiation and see if it helps you come out a winner!

It's from the forge of
failure that the steel of
success is formed.

Hard Work Does Not
Guarantee Success, But
Success Does Not Happen
Without Hard Work.

- Dr. Jim Anderson

Create An Effective Negotiating Team At Your Company!

Dr. Jim Anderson is available to provide training and coaching on the topics that are the most important to people who have to negotiate: how can my team effectively prepare for and execute a successful negotiation that will get us what we both want and need?

Dr. Anderson believes that in order to both learn and remember what he says, audiences need to laugh. Each one of his speeches is full of fun and humor so that what he says "sticks" with everyone.

Dr. Anderson's Negotiating Training Includes:

1. How to plan for a negotiation: what information do you need and where can you find it?

2. What's the best way to explore how a deal can be created during a negotiation?

3. How can you bring a negotiation to a close without giving in to the other side?

Dr. Jim Anderson works with over 100 customers per year. To invite Dr. Anderson to work with you, contact him at:

Phone: 813-418-6970 or
Email: jim@BlueElephantConsulting.com

Blue
Elephant
Consulting

Speaking   Negotiating   Managing   Market

Photo Credits:

Cover – cutiepie company

https://www.flickr.com/photos/cutiepiecompany/

Chapter 1 - coconinoco
https://www.flickr.com/photos/coconino/

Chapter 2 - Ben Schumin

https://www.flickr.com/photos/schuminweb/

Chapter 3 - e r j k . a m e r j k a

https://www.flickr.com/photos/24842486@N07/

Chapter 4 - Daniel Slaughter

https://www.flickr.com/photos/danielslaughter/

Chapter 5 - Rilind Hoxha

https://www.flickr.com/photos/rilindh/

Chapter 6 - Philippe Put

https://www.flickr.com/photos/34547181@N00/

Chapter 7 - Amancay Maahs

https://www.flickr.com/photos/amanky/

Chapter 8 - rubyblossom.

https://www.flickr.com/photos/rubyblossom/

Chapter 9 - AJC1

https://www.flickr.com/photos/ajc1/

Chapter 10 - Tony Hall

https://www.flickr.com/photos/anotherphotograph/

Chapter 11 – mahjqa

https://www.flickr.com/photos/28134808@N02/

Chapter 12 – David

https://www.flickr.com/photos/randomcuriosity/

Other Books By The Author

Product Management

- How Product Managers Can Sell More Of Their Product: Tips & Techniques For Product Managers To Better Understand How To Sell Their Product

- How Product Managers Can Sell More Of Their Product: Tips & Techniques For Product Managers To Better Understand How To Sell Their Product

- How To Create A Successful Product That Customers Will Want: Techniques For Product Managers To Boost Product Sales And Increase Customer Satisfaction

- What Product Managers Need To Know About World-Class Product Development: How Product Managers Can Create Successful Products

- How Product Managers Can Learn To Understand Their Customers: Techniques For Product Managers To Better Understand What Their Customers Really Want

- Product Management Secrets: Techniques For Product Managers To Boost Product Sales And Increase Customer Satisfaction

- Product Development Lessons For Product Managers: How Product Managers Can Create Successful Products

- Customer Lessons For Product Managers: Techniques For Product Managers To Better Understand What Their Customers Really Want

- Product Failure Lessons For Product Managers: Examples Of Products That Have Failed For Product Managers To Learn From

- Communication Skills For Product Managers: The Communication Skills That Product Managers Need To Know How To Use In Order To Have A Successful Product

- How To Have A Successful Product Manager Career: The Things That You Need To Be Doing TODAY In Order To Have A Successful Product Manager Career

- Product Manager Product Success: How to keep your product on track and make it become a success

Public Speaking

- Creating Speeches That Work: How To Create A Speech That Will Make Your Message Be Remembered Forever!

- How To Organize A Speech In Order To Make Your Point: How to put together a speech that will capture and hold your audience's attention

- Changing How You Speak To Overcome Your Fear Of Speaking: Change techniques that will transform a speech into a memorable event

- Delivering Excellence: How To Give Presentations That Make A Difference: Presentation techniques that will transform a speech into a memorable event

- Tools Speakers Need In Order To Give The Perfect Speech: What tools to use to create your next speech so that your message will be remembered forever!

- How To Create A Speech That Will Be Remembered

- Secrets To Organizing A Speech For Maximum Impact: How to put together a speech that will capture and hold your audience's attention

- How To Become A Better Speaker By Changing How You Speak: Change techniques that will transform a speech into a memorable event

- How To Give A Great Presentation: Presentation techniques that will transform a speech into a memorable event

- How To Rehearse In Order To Give The Perfect Speech: How to effectively rehearse your next speech to that your message be remembered forever!

- Secrets To Creating The Perfect Speech: How to create a speech that will make your message be remembered forever!

- Secrets To Organizing The Perfect Speech: How to organize the best speech of your life!

- Secrets To Planning The Perfect Speech: How to plan to give the best speech of your life

- How To Show What You Mean During A Presentation: How to use visual techniques to transform a speech into a memorable event

CIO Skills

- How CIOs Can Bring Business And IT Together: How CIOs Can Use Their Technical Skills To Help Their Company Solve Real-World Business Problems

- New IT Technology Issues Facing CIOs: How CIOs Can Stay On Top Of The Changes In The Technology That Powers The Company

- Keeping The Barbarians Out: How CIOs Can Secure Their Department and Company: Tips And Techniques For CIOs To Use In Order To Secure Both Their IT Department And Their Company

- What CIOs Need To Know In Order To Successfully Manage An IT Department: Decision Making Skills That Every CIO Needs To Have In Order To Be Able To Make The Right Choices

- Becoming A Powerful And Effective Leader: Tips And Techniques That IT Managers Can Use In Order To Develop Leadership Skills

- CIO Secrets For Growing Innovation: Tips And Techniques For CIOs To Use In Order To Make Innovation Happen In Their IT Department

- Your Success As A CIO Depends On How Well You Communicate: Tips And Techniques For CIOs To

Use In Order To Become Better Communicators

- What CIOs Need To Know About Working With Partners: Techniques For CIOs To Use In Order To Be Able To Successfully Work With Partners

- Critical CIO Management Skills: Decision Making Skills That Every CIO Needs To Have In Order To Be Able To Make The Right Choices

- How CIOs Can Make Innovation Happen: Tips And Techniques For CIOs To Use In Order To Make Innovation Happen In Their IT Department

- CIO Communication Skills Secrets: Tips And Techniques For CIOs To Use In Order To Become Better Communicators

- Managing Your CIO Career: Steps That CIOs Have To Take In Order To Have A Long And Successful Career

- CIO Business Skills: How CIOs can work effectively with the rest of the company!

IT Manager Skills

- How IT Managers Can Use New Technology To Meet Today's IT Challenges: Technologies That IT

Managers Can Use In Order to Make Their Teams More Productive

- How To Build High Performance IT Teams: Tips And Techniques That IT Managers Can Use In Order To Develop Productive Teams

- Save Yourself, Save Your Job – How To Manage Your IT Career: Secrets That IT Managers Can Use In Order To Have A Successful Career

- Growing Your CIO Career: How CIOs Can Work With The Entire Company In Order To Be Successful

- How IT Managers Can Make Innovation Happen: Tips And Techniques For IT Managers To Use In Order To Make Innovation Happen In Their Teams

- Staffing Skills IT Managers Must Have: Tips And Techniques That IT Managers Can Use In Order To Correctly Staff Their Teams

- Secrets Of Effective Leadership For IT Managers: Tips And Techniques That IT Managers Can Use In Order To Develop Leadership Skills

- IT Manager Career Secrets: Tips And Techniques That IT Managers Can Use In Order To Have A

Successful Career

- IT Manager Budgeting Skills: How IT Managers Can Request, Manage, Use, And Track Their Funding

- Secrets Of Managing Budgets: What IT Managers Need To Know In Order To Understand How Their Company Uses Money

Negotiating

- Getting What You Want In A Negotiation By Learning How To Signal: How To Develop The Skill Of Effective Signaling In A Negotiation In Order To Get The Best Possible Outcome

- Exploring How To Get The Deal That You Want In A Negotiation: How To Develop The Skill Of Exploring What Is Possible In A Negotiation In Order To Reach The Best Possible Deal

- Use The Power Of Arguing To Win Your Next Negotiation: How To Develop The Skill Of Effective Arguing In A Negotiation In Order To Get The Best Possible Outcome

- Learn How To Signal In Your Next Negotiation: How To Develop The Skill Of Effective Signaling In A Negotiation In Order To Get The Best Possible

Outcome

- Learn The Skill Of Exploring In A Negotiation: How To Develop The Skill Of Exploring What Is Possible In A Negotiation In Order To Reach The Best Possible Deal

- Learn How To Argue In Your Next Negotiation: How To Develop The Skill Of Effective Arguing In A Negotiation In Order To Get The Best Possible Outcome|

- How To Open Your Next Negotiation: How To Start A Negotiation In Order To Get The Best Possible Outcome

- Preparing For Your Next Negotiation: What You Need To Do BEFORE A Negotiation Starts In Order To Get The Best Possible Deal

- Learn How To Package Trades In Your Next Negotiation

- All Good Things Come To An End: How To Close A Negotiation - How To Develop The Skill Of Closing In Order To Get The Best Possible Outcome From A Negotiation

- Take No Prisoners In Your Next Negotiation: How To Start A Negotiation In Order To Get The Best Possible Outcome

Miscellaneous

- How To Heal A Broken Leg – Fast!: Understanding how to deal with a broken leg in order to start walking again quickly

- How Software Defined Networking (SDN) Is Going To Change Your World Forever: The Revolution In Network Design And How It Affects You

- The Power Of Virtualization: How It Affects Memory, Servers, and Storage: The Revolution In Creating Virtual Devices And How It Affects You

- The Internet-Enabled Successful School District Superintendent: How To Use The Internet To Boost Parental Involvement In Your Schools

- Power Distribution Unit (PDU) Secrets: What Everyone Who Works In A Data Center Needs To Know!

- Making The Jump: How To Land Your Dream Job When You Get Out Of College!

- How To Use The Internet To Create Successful Students And Involved Parents

How To Develop The Skill Of Assembling Potential Trades In Order To Get The Best Possible Outcome

---

This book has been written with one goal in mind – to show you how to successfully package trades in your next negotiation. It's not easy being a negotiator and so we're going to show you how to successfully assemble the trades that will get you the deal that you want!

Let's Make Your Negotiation A Success!

What You'll Find Inside:

- **THE POWER OF DELAYS IN A NEGOTIATION**

- **LEARN TO THINK LONG-TERM IN YOUR NEXT NEGOTIATION**

- **WHY NEGOTIATORS SHOULD PUT A DEAD DOG ON THE TABLE**

- **WHY EVERY NEGOTIATOR SHOULD HAVE A "DEAL BOOK"**

Dr. Jim Anderson brings his 25 years of real-world experience to this book. He's been a negotiator at some of the world's largest firms. He's going to show you what you need to do (and not do!) in order to get the best deal out of your next negotiation!

.

www.ingramcontent.com/pod-product-compliance
Lightning Source LLC
Chambersburg PA
CBHW071758170526
45167CB00003B/1081